The Family Celebrates

PENTECOST

McCrimmons
Great Wakering   Essex   England

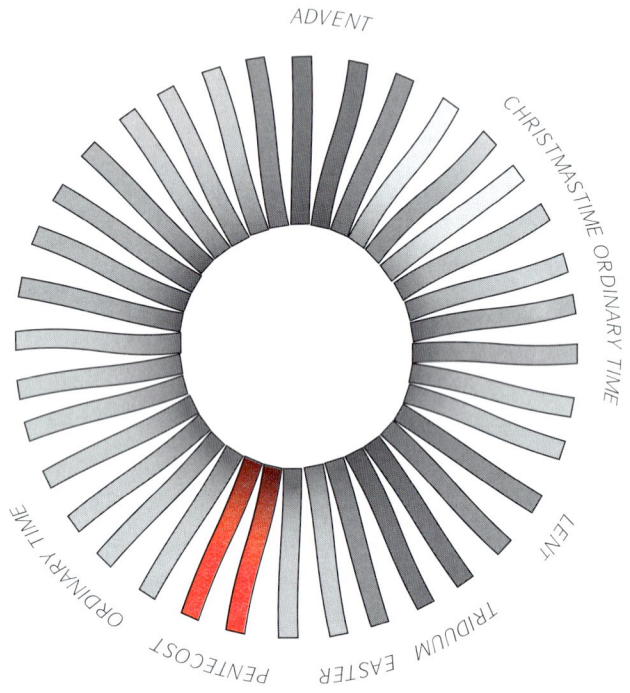

First published in 1996 in Great Britain by
McCrimmon Publishing Company Limited
10-12 High Street, Great Wakering, Essex SS3 0EQ
Telephone (01702) 218956; Fax: (01702) 216082

© 1996 Diocese of Arundel & Brighton. Joan Brown SND, Elaine Gibbs,
Elizabeth Rees OCV and Mary Travers NDS.

ISBN 0 85597 555 5

Illustrations by Gunvor Edwards
Cover design and page layout by Nick Snode
Body text set in Century Old Style 12/13.5, chapter headings set in Formal Script 421

Reprographics by Anagram Litho Ltd., Southend-on-Sea, Essex
Printed on 90gsm matt art / 240gsm Invercote
Printed by Mayhew McCrimmon Printers Ltd., Great Wakering, Essex

Contents

The Pentecost story	4
Celebrate Pentecost at Home	5
The Christian Pentecost	11
The Novena Book	14
A Pentecost Fire	15
Gifts of the Holy Spirit	17
Things to do	19
Cheesecake	
Toffee Apples	
Pentecost Mobile	
Pentecost Windmill	

The Pentecost Story

ON THE DAY of Pentecost the friends of Jesus were gathered together in the same house in Jerusalem. Suddenly a noise came from heaven. It sounded like a strong wind blowing, it filled the whole house where they were sitting.
Then they saw something that looked like flames of fire. The flames separated and rested on each person present in the room. They were all filled with the Holy Spirit and were given the power to speak in different languages. In Jerusalem at that time were Jews from every country in the world, who had come to celebrate the feast of weeks or Shavouot. The noise attracted a huge crowd. Everyone was amazed when they heard their own language being spoken. They said, 'Aren't all these men we hear speaking from Galilee, but each of us hears them in our own language. How is this possible? We are from many different countries: Parthia, Media, Elam, Mesopotamia, Judea, Cappadocia, Pontus, Asia, Phrygia, Pamphylia, Egypt, Libya, Rome, Crete, Arabia.' No one could understand what was happening, everyone was amazed and perplexed, some even made fun of the friends of Jesus and saying they must be drunk. However Peter, standing up with the eleven apostles spoke to the crowd in a loud voice saying: 'What you are seeing is the outpouring of the Holy Spirit as the prophets foretold.'

Celebrate Pentecost at Home

Introduction

Pentecost follows Easter
as summer follows springtime,
as mid-day follows sunrise.

> *'The winter is over;*
> *the rains have stopped,*
> *in the countryside the flowers are in bloom.*
> *This is the time for singing…'*
>
> Song of Songs 2: 11-12

Singing the Easter alleluia, we remember how Jesus was raised to new life, we remember how we were given new birth in the waters of baptism, we remember how, on the fortieth day after rising to new life, Jesus ascended to his Father, we remember how, on the fiftieth day, Pentecost, Jesus sent the Holy Spirit.

The Family Celebrates Pentecost

At Pentecost we celebrate the birthday of the Church.
Every year at Pentecost we remember how through the gift of the Holy Spirit we are empowered to go out to the whole world and proclaim the Good News...
    WE ARE SAVED

'God is love' and love is God's first gift, containing all others.
'God's love has been poured into our hearts through the Holy Spirit who has been given to us.' *Romans 5.5*

Grafted onto the true vine, God's children can bear much fruit by the power of the Holy Spirit... love, joy, peace, patience, kindness, goodness, faithfulness, gentleness, self-control.

'No one can say 'Jesus is Lord' except by the Holy Spirit.'
God has sent the Spirit of his Son into our hearts, crying, 'Abba! Father!' *Galatians 4.6*

Why Celebrate at Home?

Celebrations in the home can help families to live their faith as a way of life, and also help children to understand that being a Christian is something more than going to Mass on Sunday.

Many signs and symbols are woven into the liturgical celebrations of the Church, the meanings of which are not always immediately obvious.
Celebrations at home can help us to understand how they relate to Christ and are expressed in our lives.

In this book we offer ideas and suggestions for celebrating Pentecost with the family at home.
These ideas can be used as they are, adapted, or perhaps will inspire your own ideas.

Celebrate Pentecost at Home

Why is it helpful to learn about the family of Jesus?

In a relationship we like to learn as much as we can about our friend, in order to deepen our love and friendship. The closer we get to someone, the more we want to know about them; the same is also true of our relationship with Jesus.

Jesus belonged to a Jewish family. He grew up in a Jewish home where he was familiar with drawing water from the well, baking bread and helping in the carpenter's shop. His home was the place where he learnt to celebrate the festivals which recalled the history and traditions of the Jewish people.
It was against this background that his future teaching took shape.

As a boy Jesus would have enjoyed family meals, singing the ancient blessings before and after them.

Each springtime his family would prepare a Passover meal in memory of the escape from the slavery in Egypt of their Jewish ancestors: a meal which Jesus would continue to celebrate with his friends during his life. This was a celebration of freedom and fifty days (seven weeks) later they would celebrate the Feast

The Family Celebrates Pentecost

of Weeks or Shavouot to remember how God gave Moses wise laws to protect his people from harm. We call these ancient laws the Ten Commandments.

From Passover to Pentecost Jesus, like all Jewish children, would have enjoyed counting the 50 days – which is known as counting the Omer.
Even today Jewish families gather to pray and count the Omer during this time.

As we have our Advent calendars to count off the days to Christmas, from the second day of Passover for forty nine days to Pentecost Jewish families count the Omer. At Pentecost the Jewish people commemorate the giving of the Law to Moses on Mount Sinai seven weeks after the Jewish people had been set free from slavery in Egypt, which they regard as the most important event in their history.

Celebrate Pentecost at Home

Moses spent forty days with God on the mountain before returning to the people with the ten commandments.

The law is what God has revealed to us and what we have come to understand about God... The law and commandments are a way of life, the path of self-fulfilment, the design for a better world. The law is God's choice gift to the chosen people of Israel. God is present among those who study these laws. Pentecost is a joyous feast when the Jewish people thank God for having given them these wise laws. Synagogues and homes are decorated with flowers, a reminder of the early summer flowers which bloomed on Mount Sinai.

We might copy this Pentecost custom by decorating our homes, as well as our churches with flowers and greenery for Pentecost.

The Christian Pentecost

Pentecost is the Greek word for fifty days.
For fifty days after Jesus rose from the dead his friends waited anxiously in Jerusalem, wondering what would happen next. Then something powerful happened. The Spirit of Jesus filled them with new life and energy. They felt on fire with God's Spirit. Each one felt a new flame of life lighting them up from the inside. St Luke says God's Spirit blew into their house like a powerful wind, like dancing flames of fire. Each person felt a flame of fire, it gave them new warmth and light.

Wind and fire are ancient symbols to describe how God is present. At the foot of Mount Sinai, where he was looking after the sheep, Moses met God when he came upon a blazing bush. As he looked at the burning bush God spoke to him. From early Christian times to this very day Orthodox Monks, who live at the foot of Mount Sinai have carefully tended a giant bramble bush which traditionally represents the burning bush.

The Christian Pentecost

At the feast of Pentecost Jewish people serve a meal of dairy products such as cheese cakes and milk and honey and pancakes stuffed with cheese, because until the people got to know God's law they were not sure about how they should prepare meat, so they ate dairy foods.
The tradition to eat dairy foods at Pentecost reminds them that God's law is nourishing and sweet like milk and honey.

You might celebrate Pentecost with some of your favourite foods containing these ingredients, like milk shakes, ice cream, treacle tart.

To help children understand that the giving of the Spirit concerns us not only when we are in Church, but throughout the whole of our lives, you can have a Pentecost celebration at home based on the symbols of wind and fire, signs of the power of God's presence in our lives. In many countries people celebrate God's power and presence by building a summer bonfire. They sing and dance around it to share their happiness.

Perhaps you could build a Pentecost bonfire in your garden with friends or have a barbecue and celebrate with sparklers.

The Family Celebrates Pentecost

Another idea might be to organise a family picnic and make some kites to fly or at least have some windmills for smaller children to run around with.

For children much of the fun of a celebration is in the preparation and the excitement of anticipation. Just as we have the two vigils, Advent and Lent, of waiting and preparing for Christmas and Easter, in memory of the time when the Apostles in Jerusalem waited for the coming of God's Spirit, we have the novena for Pentecost – nine days of prayer which has been a custom in the church since earliest times, beginning on the day following Ascension day and ending on Pentecost Sunday. Children can be introduced to a simple form of novena to the Holy Spirit and they can make and illustrate their own novena book with nine pages, one for each day.

Perhaps counting the days from Easter to the Ascension could blossom into the novena, highlighting the connection between the feasts.

The Novena Book

On the cover write GOD IS LIKE …
Decorate the cover beautifully.

Complete one page each day for nine days.
Make a picture of something we learn about God from wind and fire.

Examples

God is like: a powerful wind
a gentle breeze
a powerful storm
a warming fire
a candle lighting up the darkness
fireworks
a blazing forest fire…

Encourage the children to think up their own images.
Older children may be able to write about their illustrations or add a prayer.

On the last page draw a picture of the Pentecost story when God's Spirit rushed like wind into the room where the friends of Jesus were waiting, dancing over each person's head like a flame of fire.

A Pentecost Fire

On the night before Pentecost, Whitsun Eve, prepare a bonfire and/or light a barbecue. Bring torches and/or sparklers.

Light the bonfire and sing, 'Colours of day.'
Each time you sing the chorus:

> 'Then light up the fire
> And let the flame burn,
> Open the door
> Let Jesus return…'

walk round the fire clapping your hands.

A Pentecost Fire

Read the Pentecost story...

Words from the
Acts of the Apostles

> On the day of Pentecost the friends of Jesus were gathered together in the same house in Jerusalem. Suddenly a noise came from heaven. It sounded like a strong wind blowing, it filled the whole house where they were sitting. Then they saw something that looked like flames of fire. The flames separated and rested on each person present in the room.
>
> This is the word of the Lord.

Light the sparklers or torches.
Make beautiful patterns of light in the air
Write the name GOD in light with your torches or sparklers.
Write your own name.
As the fire dies down eat your barbecued food and watch the glowing embers.
Enjoy the beauty of the fire.

Gifts of the Holy Spirit

The Holy Spirit gives us many gifts which help us to be happy. Here are seven of them:

Wisdom...
being sensible.

Understanding...
learning about things.

Counsel...
giving good advice.

Fortitude...
being brave

Knowledge...
knowing about things

Piety...
remembering God loves you.

Gifts of the Holy Spirit

Wonder of God…
    living close to God.

You might like to ask the Holy Spirit for one or more gifts on Pentecost day.

Things to do

Here are some recipes you might like to try.

CHEESECAKE

Ingredients

5 digestive-type biscuits
125gms margarine or butter
125gms sugar
$^1/_2$ teaspoon vanilla essence
1 teaspoon lemon juice
2 eggs
500gms cottage cheese
2 level tablespoons self-raising flour
4 tablespoons single cream
250ml sour cream
1 tablespoon sugar (optional)

Method

Grease a 20cm loose bottomed tin. Sprinkle with crushed biscuits. Cream fat and sugar together. Beat in vanilla and lemon juice. Beat in the eggs. Beat in the cottage cheese and sifted flour. Beat in the single cream.
Place mixture on the biscuits in the cake tin
Bake at 350°F, gas mark 4, centre of the oven,
$1\,^1/_4$ to $1\,^1/_2$ hours

Mix together sour cream and sugar, spread over the cake when cool. Refrigerate until served.

Things to do

TOFFEE APPLES

Ingredients *(for twelve apples)*

    5 tablespoons water
    100gms honey
    2 teaspoons vinegar
    450gms granulated sugar
    50gms butter

Method

Pour water and honey into a pan and bring to the boil
Remove from heat and add vinegar, butter, sugar stirring all the time. Heat slowly until butter and sugar are melted
Bring to the boil and boil gently for 2 minutes.

Turn down the heat and continue to boil for 15 more minutes 138°C / 280°F. Push a stick into each apple then dip apples into the toffee mixture.
Leave to cool on a greased tray.

Things to do

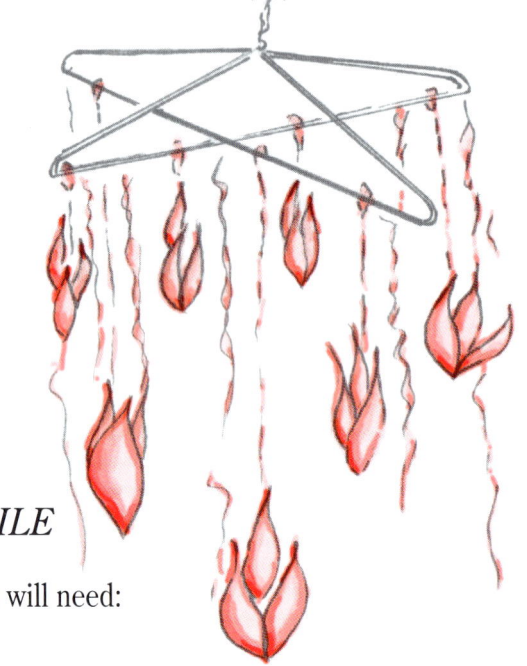

PENTECOST MOBILE

The make the mobile you will need:

> 2 wire coat hangers
> Reel of thread
> Cellotape
> Scissors
> Strips of cellophane
> Several flames cut from metallic paper

Instructions

> Fasten the coat hangers together crosswise.
> Use the thread to suspend the flames at different heights from the coat hangers.
> Cut the cellophane into strips of different lengths and cellotape to hang down from the coat hangers.
>
> Hang your finished mobile where there is a current of air.

Things to do

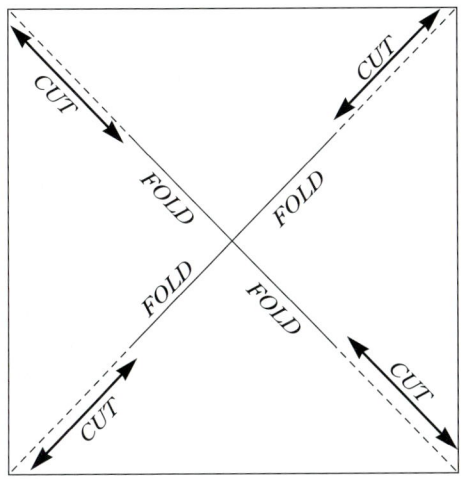

PENTECOST WINDMILL

For a Pentecost windmill, fold a square of paper diagonally and cut as shown in the diagram. Draw the four points to the centre and put a pin through them, then through a bead and finally into a wooden handle such as a ruler.
Blowing on the blades will make the pinwheel go round.

Make them at Pentecost before telling how the Spirit comes like a rushing wind.

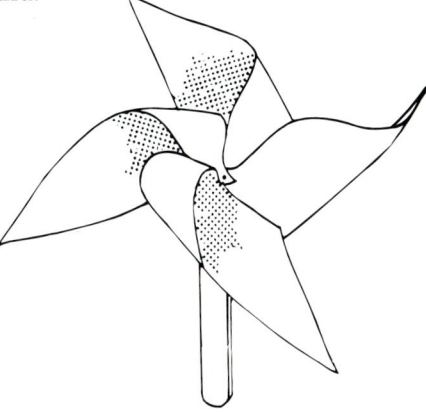

The Family Celebrates Series

The Family Celebrates Advent	0 85597 561 X
The Family Celebrates Christmas	0 85597 562 8
The Family Celebrates Lent	0 85597 564 4
The Family Celebrates Easter	0 85597 554 7
The Family Celebrates Pentecost	0 85597 555 5
The Family Celebrates Autumn	0 85597 563 6
Autumn will contain	
Harvest	
All Saints	
The Family Celebrates All Souls	0 85597 568 7
All Souls will contain	
Christ the King	
The Family Celebrates with Mary	0 85597 565 2
The Family Celebrates Feasts of our Lord	0 85597 567 9
The Family Celebrates Reconciliation	0 85597 569 5
The Family Goes to Church	0 85597 570 9